Learning Short-take®

ADULT LEARNING PRINCIPLES 1

Understanding the ways adults learn

CATHERINE MATTISKE

TPC - The Performance Company Pty Ltd
Level 20, Darling Park
Tower 2, 201 Sussex Street,
Sydney NSW 2000
Australia

ACN 077 455 273
email: tpc@tpc.net.au
Website: www.catherinemattiske.com

© TPC – The Performance Company Pty Limited
First edition published in 2006
Second edition published in 2017
Third edition published in 2022

All rights reserved. Apart from any fair dealing for the purposes of study, research or review, as permitted under Australian copyright law, no part of this publication may be reproduced by any means without the written permission of the copyright owner. Every effort has been made to obtain permission relating to information reproduced in this publication.

The information in this publication is based on the current state of commercial and industry practice, applicable legislation, general law and the general circumstances as at the date of publication. No person shall rely on any of the contents of this publication and the publisher and the author expressly exclude all liability for direct and indirect loss suffered by any person resulting in any way from the use of or reliance on this publication or any part of it. Any options and advice are offered solely in pursuance of the author's and the publisher's intention to provide information, and have not been specifically sought.

For eBook version: By payment of the required fees, you have been granted the non-exclusive, non-transferable right to access and read the text of this e-book on screen. No part of this text may be reproduced, transmitted, downloaded, decompiled, reverse engineered, or stored in or introduced into any information storage retrieval system, in any form or by any means, whether the electronic or mechanical, now known or hereinafter invented, without the express permission of the author.

 A catalogue record for this book is available from the National Library of Australia

National Library of Australia
Cataloguing-in-Publication data

Mattiske, Catherine
Adult Learning Principles 1: Understanding the Ways Adults Learn

ISBN 978-1-921547-00-3

1. Occupational training 2. Learning I. Title

370.113

Distributed by TPC - The Performance Company - www.catherinemattiske.com
For further information contact TPC - The Performance Company, Sydney Australia on +61 (02) 9555 1953.

HELLO.

Welcome to the Learning Short-take® process!

This Learning Short-take® is a bite sized learning package that aims to improve your skills and provide you with an opportunity for personal and professional development to achieve success in your role.

This Learning Short-take® combines self study with workplace activities in a unique learning system to keep you motivated and energized.
So let's get started!

Step 1:
What's inside?

- Learning Short-take®. This section contains all of the learning content and will guide you through the learning process.
- Learning Activities. You will be prompted to complete these as you read through.
- Learning Journal. Update your Learning Journal at the end of each section when prompted.
- Skill Development Action Plan. Learning is about taking action. This is your action plan where you'll plan how you will implement your learning.

Step 2:
Complete the Learning Short-take®

- Learning Short-takes® are best completed in a quiet environment that is free of distractions.
- Schedule time in your calendar to complete the Learning Short-take® and prioritize this time as an investment in your own professional development.
- Depending on the title, most participants complete the Learning Short-take® from 90 minutes to 2.5 hours.

Step 3:
Meet with your Manager/Coach

- Schedule a 30 minute meeting with your Manager or Coach.
- At this meeting share your completed Activities, Learning Journal and Skill Development Action Plan.
- Most importantly, discuss and agree on how you will implement your learning in your role.

GET VIP ACCESS TO YOUR MATERIALS

This Learning Short-take® includes an interactive activity book, associated tools and job aids, plus a bonus eBook.

1 Visit https://www.catherinemattiske.com/books

2 Select your book

3 Click: VIP ACCESS

4 Enter the code: ALP12022046

WELCOME

Adult Learning Principles 1
Understanding the Ways Adults Learn

Adult Learning Principles 1 combines self-study with realistic workplace activities for trainers, educators, facilitators and managers to develop skills and knowledge in the principles of adult learning. It will add adult learning techniques to your 'grab bag' of learning design tools for improved learning outcomes. After evaluation of your current approach to learning design, you will learn to develop new and innovative strategies to engage learners at every level. Significantly increasing participant retention and training results **Adult Learning Principles 1** will fuel your confidence in designing successful training workshops and e-Learning every time.

The principles of adult learning work on the basis that we all learn differently, and the way we like to receive and interpret information varies from person to person. Trainers and facilitators who use a combination of adult learning principles to provide balance in their programs increase the chances of keeping all participants focused and engaged throughout the learning process. **Adult Learning Principles 1** will assist you in building a good mix of adult learning styles which is critical in ensuring learning, thorough participant retention and workplace application.

Adult Learning Principles 1 includes the job aid **Strategies for Meeting Global and Specific Needs**, the **Adult Learning Principles Quick Reference Wall Chart** and **the Activity Booklet,** provided as free downloadable tools.

Now let's get started!

1	Learning Short-take® >	Start here
2	Learning Journal	55
3	Skill Development Action Plan	61
4	Quick Reference	67
5	Next Steps	87

"It's what you learn after you know it all that counts."

JOHN WOODEN

"

*The most useful piece of learning for the uses
of life is to unlearn what is untrue.*

ANTISTHENES

Section 1
LEARNING SHORT-TAKE®

WHAT'S IN THIS LEARNING SHORT-TAKE®

"You can teach a student a lesson for a day; but if you can teach him to learn by creating curiosity, he will continue the learning process as long as he lives."

CLAY P. BEDFORD

Table of Contents

How to Complete Your Learning Short-take®	5
Activity Checklist	6
Learning Objectives	7
Let's Get Started	13
Part 1 - Understanding Adult Learners	15
Three Adult Learning Principles	18
Part 2 - Adult Learning Principles - Global versus Specific Learners	19
More on Global and Specific - General Notes	25
Part 3 - Adult Learning Principles - Learning Style - Modalities	31
Part 4 - Adult Learning Principles - Learning Types - The 4Mat System	43
The 4Mat Model in More Detail	46
Part 5 - Major Review	51
Summary of Key Points	52

HOW TO COMPLETE YOUR LEARNING SHORT-TAKE®

1. **Reflect on your skills and abilities** in knowing how you learn and then transferring that knowledge to the needs of your learners.

2. **Complete the Initial Skills Self-Assessment**.

3. Highlight specific skill areas that you believe you could develop more. Add these to the **Learning Journal**. Add to your Learning Journal as you go.

4. When you have completed this Learning Short-take® **meet with your Manager/Coach**. In this meeting, you will jointly establish a personal **Skill Development Action Plan**.

5. **Subject to your Manager's or Coach's final review** and assessment, you will either sign off the Learning Short-take®, or undertake further skill development as appropriate.

"Success is not forever; and failure isn't fatal."

DON SHULA

ACTIVITY CHECKLIST

"In the spider-web of facts, many a truth is strangled."

PAUL ELDRIDGE

During this Learning Short-take® you will be prompted to complete the following activities:

- Activity 1 - Initial Skills Self-Assessment   8
- Activity 2 - Key Terms of Adult Learning   10
- Activity 3 - Global versus Specific   23
- Activity 4 - Learning Styles - Modalities - What's What?   34
- Activity 5 - Learning Style Preference   38
- Activity 6a - Learning Style & Task Association   40
- Activity 6b - Learning Style Ideas Generation   42
- Activity 7 - Learning Types Ideas Generation   48
- Activity 8 - Final Review - True or False   53
- Learning Journal   55
- Skill Development Action Plan   61

LEARNING OBJECTIVES

After you have completed this Learning Short-take®, you should be able to:

- Successfully match adult learning terms with definitions
- Determine your personal Learning Style preference
- List and give working examples of three Adult Learning Principles - Global versus Specific, Learning Styles and Learning Types
- Develop strategies and ideas to link Adult Learning Principles with Instructional Design.

Complete Activity # 1
Initial Skills Self-Assessment

Complete Activity # 2
Key Terms of Adult Learning

ACTIVITY 1: INITIAL SKILLS SELF-ASSESSMENT

Understanding Adult Learning Principles is critical to participant retention and application of new skills and knowledge. This assessment covers the core skills in developing training programs and delivering training in a corporate environment to maximize learning transfer.

Rate yourself on each of the techniques.
7 is competent and confident, little need for improvement
4 is average, needs improvement
1 is uncomfortable, major need for improvement

- Note specific areas of improvement related to each training delivery or instructional design skill that you would like to develop. Be sure to include your reasons for your rating in each skill, as this reasoning will be a key part of the initial goal setting session with your coach.
- Start thinking about a Personal Development Plan and identify two things you could do to improve your skills in this area and write them in the space provided.

I...	Rating
1. incorporate an agenda or overview at the beginning of every training program	1 2 3 4 5 6 7
2. clearly list objectives for every training program	1 2 3 4 5 6 7
3. summarize and review each topic after it is presented before moving onto the next topic	1 2 3 4 5 6 7
4. use lists and clear step-by-step processes within the course material	1 2 3 4 5 6 7
5. back up opinion with referenced facts	1 2 3 4 5 6 7
6. use color and pictures on visual aids	1 2 3 4 5 6 7

ACTIVITY 1: CONTINUED

I...	Rating
7. incorporate activities such as group discussion and teach-backs	1 2 3 4 5 6 7
8. ensure participants are physically moving regularly throughout the training program	1 2 3 4 5 6 7
9. include opportunities for participants to practice new skills	1 2 3 4 5 6 7
10. outline the benefits of each topic before launching into the content	1 2 3 4 5 6 7
11. clearly state facts and details in a logical sequential manner	1 2 3 4 5 6 7
12. provide practical examples of how the topic can be applied	1 2 3 4 5 6 7
13. give tips, tricks and traps on real-life situations regarding implementation of content	1 2 3 4 5 6 7

Personal development plan ideas:

1

2

Now update your Learning Journal (page 55)

ACTIVITY 2: KEY TERMS OF ADULT LEARNING

Activity – Terms and Definition Match

Draw a line to match each term in the left column to the correct definition in the right column. Then, check your work on page 12!

Training Purpose — A learning theory relating to the approach to learning by adults. One group need to see the 'big picture', the overview and the end goal of the learning. The other group of learners (also known as linear learners) require detail and specifics, sometimes without regard for the end-goal.

Global & Specific — A general term relating to adult learning style on the sensory intake of information. People learn through their 5 senses (touch, sight, hearing, taste and smell) and this term in adult learning is known as 'modalities'.

Content Expertise — A general term relating to adult learning style on how information is learned. This term is underpinned by research conducted by Bernice McCarthy who has developed the 4-Mat system.

Orchestration — The extensive knowledge of a discipline and an equally important love for the content of that discipline. (You should have this about your content area)

Learning Style — The personal presence necessary to organize a group of participants, with the flow necessary for successful timing, never outdistancing, never allowing stagnation.

Learning Type — The three outcomes of training are to **increase** knowledge, skill and or attitude, **retain** the learning and **apply** the learning.

"Whatever you can do or dream you can - begin it. Boldness has genius, power and magic."

JOHANN WOLFGANG VON GOETHE

Activity 2 - Check your Answers

Check your answers from the previous section

Content Expertise	The extensive knowledge of a discipline and an equally important love for the content of that discipline. (You should have this about your content area)
Orchestration	The personal presence necessary to organize a group of participants, with the flow necessary for successful timing, never outdistancing, never allowing stagnation.
Learning Style	A general term relating to adult learning style on the sensory intake of information. People learn through their 5 senses (touch, sight, hearing, taste and smell) and this term in adult learning is known as 'modalities'.
Learning Type	A general term relating to adult learning style on how information is learned. This term is underpinned by research conducted by Bernice McCarthy who has developed the 4Mat system.
Global & Specific	A learning theory relating to the approach to learning by adults. One group need to see the 'big picture', the overview and the end goal of the learning. The other group of learners (also known as linear learners) require detail and specifics, sometimes without regard for the end-goal.
Training Purpose	The three outcomes of training are to **increase** knowledge, skill and or attitude, **retain** the learning and **apply** the learning.

Now update your Learning Journal (page 55)

LET'S GET STARTED

Adult Learners in a corporate learning environment have their own unique preferences for retaining and applying new information. When a trainer aligns their training style to the preferred learning style of participants retention and application is increased.

The goal of this Learning Short-take® is for you to build your knowledge about adult learning and then apply your skills to both the instructional design and training delivery process. Having a sound knowledge of Adult Learning Principles is a critical element of great training.

"You learn something every day if you pay attention."

RAY LEBLOND

"

We learn more by looking for the answer to a question and not finding it than we do from learning the answer itself.

LLOYD ALEXANDER

"

UNDERSTANDING ADULT LEARNERS

PART 1

UNDERSTANDING ADULT LEARNERS

Overview of Adult Learning

Adult learning is frequently spoken of by adult educators as if it were a discretely separate domain, having little association with what actually occurs in the corporate training classroom. The thinking instructional designer and trainer ensures that the 'theory' of adult learning is transferred into 'reality' during each corporate training intervention.

Learning vs Memory

Learning can be defined formally as the act, process, or experience of gaining knowledge or skills. In contrast, memory can define the capacity of storing, retrieving, and acting on that knowledge. Learning helps us move from novices to experts and allows us to gain new knowledge and abilities.

Learning strengthens the brain by building new pathways and increasing connections that we can rely on when we want to learn more. Definitions that are more complex add words such as comprehension and mastery through experience or study.

Physiology of Learning

Physiologically, learning is the formation of *cell assemblies* and *phase sequences*. Children learn by building these assemblies and sequences. Adults spend more time making new arrangements than forming new sequences. Our experience and background allow us to learn new concepts.

At the neurological level, any established knowledge (from experience and background) appears to be made up of exceedingly intricate arrangements of cell materials, electrical charges, and chemical elements. Learning requires energy; re-learning and un-learning requires even more. We must access higher brain functions to generate the much-needed energy and unbind the old.

Lifelong Learning

Remarkably, people can learn from the moment of birth. Learning can and should be a lifelong process. Learning shouldn't be defined by what happened early in life or only at school. We constantly make sense of our experiences and consistently search for meaning. In essence, we continue to learn.

In today's business environment, finding better ways to learn will propel organizations forward. Strong minds fuel strong organizations. We must capitalize on our natural styles and then build systems to satisfy needs. Only through an individual learning process can we re-create our environments and ourselves.

THREE ADULT LEARNING PRINCIPLES

Balance 'Global and Specific'

Use Multi-sensory ways of learning for each 'Learning Style'

Write for each 'Learning Type'

ADULT LEARNING PRINCIPLE 1 - GLOBAL VERSUS SPECIFIC LEARNERS

PART 2

ADULT LEARNING PRINCIPLES - GLOBAL VERSUS SPECIFIC LEARNERS

Global Thinking

Global thinkers (sometimes called "strategic thinkers") are more comfortable with new information if they can put it into context with the big picture. They also tend to be impatient with linear subjects or linear-oriented instruction since they prefer to be exposed to all the information up front so they can relate it to their overall goals.

Global Learners…

- prefer learning by observing the larger picture.
- prefer learning in great expanses rather than detail.
- learn in chunks.
- often incur no connectivity between the chunks.
- are holistic.
- may have difficulty in verbalizing processes.

Specific or Linear Thinking

Specific or Linear thinkers prefer a very structured approach to learning. For example, if a learning process involves progressive steps (such as Step A, Step B, Step C, etc.) linear thinkers will feel more comfortable starting Step B only after Step A has been fully completed. Mathematics, accounting and many sciences are considered linear subjects since they involve a more process-oriented presentation of information

Specific Learners...

- are often known as sequential learners.
- are logical.
- are stepwise - able to work systematically through step-by-step information, often without the end goal in mind.
- prefer presentation of materials in a linear and orderly manner.
- prefer instructions by incremental steps.

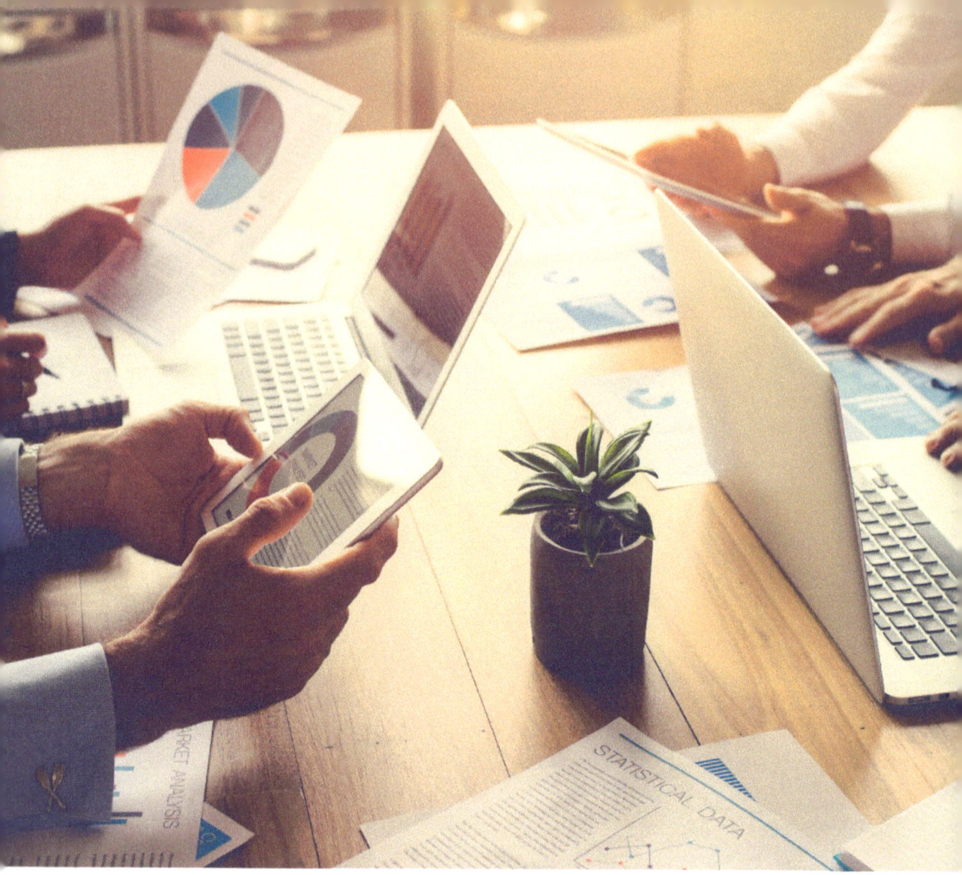

Every act of conscious learning requires the willingness to suffer an injury to one's self-esteem. That is why young children, before they are aware of their own self-importance, learn so easily.

THOMAS SZASZ

Complete Activity # 3
Global versus Specific

ACTIVITY 3: GLOBAL VERSUS SPECIFIC

From the following list of training terms, **highlight** the GLOBAL items.

- Agenda
- Big Picture Overview
- Computer keystrokes
- Content List
- Data
- Instructions
- Learning Objectives
- Overview of a course topic
- Procedures
- Process Overview
- Review Activity
- Step-by-step instructions
- Welcome
- Order

Activity 3 - Check your Answers

"I am learning all the time. The tombstone will be my diploma."

EARTHA KITT

From the previous activity - you should have highlighted the following **GLOBAL** items:

- **Agenda**
- **Big Picture Overview**
- Computer Keystrokes
- **Content List**
- Data
- Instructions
- **Learning Objectives**
- **Overview of a course topic**
- Procedures
- **Process Overview**
- **Review Activity**
- Step-by-step Instructions
- **Welcome**
- Order

Now update your Learning Journal (page 55)

MORE ON GLOBAL AND SPECIFIC - GENERAL NOTES
Comparing Global and Specific Learners

- Specific learners tend to gain understanding in linear steps, with each step following logically from the previous one. Global learners tend to learn in large jumps, absorbing material almost randomly without seeing connections, and then suddenly "getting it."

- Specific learners tend to follow logical stepwise paths in finding solutions; global learners may be able to solve complex problems quickly or put things together in novel ways once they have grasped the big picture, but they may have difficulty explaining how they did it.

Many people who read this description may conclude incorrectly that they are global, since everyone has experienced bewilderment followed by a sudden flash of understanding. What makes you global or not is what happens before the light bulb goes on. Specific learners may not fully understand the material but they can nevertheless do something with it (like solve the homework problems or pass the test) since the pieces they have absorbed are logically connected. Strongly global learners who lack good specific thinking abilities, on the other hand, may have serious difficulties until they have the big picture. Even after they have it, they may be fuzzy about the details of the subject, while specific learners may know a lot about specific aspects of a subject but may have trouble relating them to different aspects of the same subject or to different subjects.

"Learning is a treasure that will follow its owner everywhere."

CHINESE PROVERB

How can Specific Learners help themselves?

Most courses are taught in a specific manner. However, if you are a specific learner and you have a trainer who jumps around from topic to topic or skips steps, you may have difficulty following and remembering.

Ask the trainer to fill in the skipped steps, or fill them in yourself by consulting references. When you are studying, take the time to outline the lecture material for yourself in logical order. In the long run doing so will save you time.

You might also try to strengthen your global thinking skills by relating each new topic you study to things you already know. The more you can do so, the deeper your understanding of the topic is likely to be.

How can Global Learners help themselves?

If you are a global learner, it can be helpful for you to realize that you need the big picture of a subject before you can master details. If your instructor plunges directly into new topics without bothering to explain how they relate to what you already know, it can cause problems for you. Fortunately, there are steps you can take that may help you get the big picture more rapidly.

Before you begin to study the first section of a chapter in a text, skim through the entire chapter to get an overview. Doing so may be time-consuming initially but it may save you from going over and over individual parts later. Instead of spending a short time on every subject every night, you might find it more productive to immerse yourself in individual subjects for large blocks. Try to relate the subject to things you already know, either by asking the instructor to help you see connections or by consulting references. Above all, don't lose faith in yourself; you will eventually understand the new material, and once you do your understanding of how it connects to other topics and disciplines may enable you to apply it constructively.

Identifying a Specific Learner

Specific Strengths

- details
- focus
- organization
- remembering specifics
- direct answers
- consistency
- sense of justice
- objectivity
- individual competition
- doing one thing at a time

What you should know about the Specific style

- likes things ordered in a step-by-step way
- pays close attention to details
- must be prepared
- needs to know what to expect
- often values facts over feelings
- prefers to finish one thing at a time
- rarely becomes personally or emotionally involved
- logical
- self-motivated
- finds the facts but sometimes misses the main idea

What frustrates a Specific Learner?

- having opinion expressed as fact
- not understanding the purpose for doing something
- not understanding how they are graded
- listening to an overview without knowing all the steps involved
- dealing with generalities
- having to find personal meaning in all that they learn
- not finishing one task before going on to the next

Identifying a Global Learner

Global Strengths

- seeing the big picture
- seeing relationships
- cooperating in group efforts
- reading between the lines
- seeing many options
- sense of fairness
- paraphrasing
- doing several things at once
- reading body language
- getting others involved

What you should know about the Global style

- sensitive to other people's feelings
- flexible
- goes with the flow
- learns by discussion and working with others
- needs reassurance and reinforcement
- works hard to please others
- takes all criticism personally
- avoids individual competition
- tries to avoid conflict
- may skip steps and details

What frustrates a global learner?

- having to explain themselves analytically
- not getting a chance to explain themselves at all
- not knowing the meaning for doing something
- having to go step-by-step without knowing where they'll end up
- not being able to relate what they are learning to their own life
- not receiving enough credit for their effort
- accepting criticism without taking it personally
- people who are insensitive to other people's feelings

Download the summary job aid Strategies for Meeting Global and Specific Needs from
https://www.catherinematttiske.com/books

Sometimes I've believed as many as six impossible things before breakfast.

LEWIS CARROLL

ADULT LEARNING PRINCIPLE 2
- LEARNING STYLE
- MODALITIES

PART 3

ADULT LEARNING PRINCIPLES - LEARNING STYLE - MODALITIES

There are three types of learning styles based on the sensory intake' of information. **Auditory** learners learn best by hearing the material. **Visual** learners need to see the material to learn most effectively. **Kinesthetic** learners are those who learn best by doing.

Most individuals use a combination of all three modalities. For example, if an individual is a strong visual learner but has good listening skills, too, that person may want to use those secondary auditory skills to boost the visual modality for even better learning. The kinesthetic response of rewriting notes after the lecture will help reinforce material presented. The way in which an individual takes in new information, sorts, retains, retrieves, and reproduces it is heavily dependent on the style of learning.

Auditory Learners: *learn through listening...*

They learn best through verbal lectures, discussions, talking things through and listening to what others have to say. Auditory learners interpret the underlying meanings of speech through listening to tone of voice, pitch, speed and other nuances. Written information may have little meaning until it is heard. These learners often benefit from reading text aloud and using a recorder.

Visual Learners: *learn through seeing...*

These learners may need to see the trainer's body language and facial expression to fully understand the content of a lesson. They tend to prefer sitting at the front of the classroom to avoid visual obstructions (e.g. people's heads). They may think in pictures and learn best from visual displays including: diagrams, illustrated text books, overhead transparencies, PowerPoint presentations, videos, flipcharts and handouts. During a lecture or classroom discussion, visual learners often prefer to take detailed notes to absorb the information.

Kinesthetic Learners: *learn through, moving, doing and touching...*

Kinesthetic/Tactile learners learn best through a hands-on approach, actively exploring the physical world around them. They may find it hard to sit still for long periods and may become distracted by their need for activity and exploration.

Complete Activity # 4
Learning Styles - Modalities - What's What?

ACTIVITY 4: LEARNING STYLES – MODALITIES – WHAT'S WHAT?

Identify each item ✔ on the list as being Visual, Auditory or Kinesthetic style of learning.

	V	A	K
▪ Ask for written directions.			
▪ Color code to organize notes and possessions.			
▪ Engage in experiential learning (making models, doing lab work, and role playing).			
▪ Express abilities through dance or drama.			
▪ Have review questions or directions read aloud or recorded.			
▪ Learn by interviewing or by participating in discussions.			
▪ Memorize or drill while walking or moving.			
▪ Take frequent breaks in study periods.			
▪ Trace or copy letters and words to remember facts.			
▪ Use computer to reinforce learning through sense of touch.			
▪ Use flow charts and diagrams for note taking.			
▪ Use graphics to reinforce learning: films, slides, illustrations, diagrams and doodles.			
▪ Use recordings for reading and for lecture notes.			
▪ Visualize spelling of words or facts to be memorized.			

"When the student is ready, the teacher appears."

BUDDHIST PROVERB

HOT TIP: Note this page as a handy reference to help boost your training activity 'Ideas Bank'

Activity 4 - Check your Answers

Ensure that you have the following answers to the previous activity.

Visual Learners Should:

- Ask for written directions.
- Color code to organize notes and possessions.
- Use flow charts and diagrams for note taking.
- Use graphics to reinforce learning: films, slides, illustrations, diagrams and doodles.
- Visualize spelling of words or facts to be memorized.

Auditory Learner Should:

- Have review questions or directions read aloud or recorded.
- Learn by interviewing or by participating in discussions.
- Use recordings for reading and for class and lecture notes.

Kinesthetic Learners Should:

- Engage in experiential learning (making models, doing lab work, and role playing).
- Express abilities through dance or drama.
- Memorize or drill while walking or moving.
- Take frequent breaks in study periods.
- Trace or copy letters and words to remember facts.
- Use computer to reinforce learning through sense of touch.

Now update your Learning Journal (page 55)

 **Complete Activity # 5**
Learning Style Preference

 **Complete Activity # 6a**
Learning Style & Task Association

 **Complete Activity # 6b**
Learning Style Ideas Generation

"Learning is defined as a change in behavior. You haven't learned a thing until you can take action and use it."

DON SHULA AND KEN BLANCHARD

ACTIVITY 5: LEARNING STYLE PREFERENCE

Read each statement and select the appropriate number response as it applies to you.

> Often like you = 3
> Sometimes like you = 2
> Seldom/never like you = 1

Visual Modality

_____ I remember information better if I write it down.
_____ Looking at the person helps keep me focused.
_____ I need a quiet place to get my work done.
_____ When I take a test, I can see the textbook page in my head.
_____ I need to write down directions, not just take them verbally.
_____ Music or background noise distracts my attention from the task at hand.
_____ I do not always get the meaning of a joke.
_____ I doodle and draw pictures on the margins of my notebook pages.
_____ I have trouble following lectures.
_____ I react very strongly to colors.

_____ **Total**

Auditory Modality

_____ My papers and notebooks always seem messy.
_____ When I read, I need to use my index finger to track my place on the line.
_____ I do not follow written directions well.
_____ If I hear something, I will remember it.
_____ Writing has always been difficult for me.
_____ I often misread words from the text.
_____ I would rather listen and learn than read and learn.
_____ I'm not very good at interpreting someone's body language.
_____ Pages with small print or poor quality copies are difficult for me to read.
_____ My eyes tire quickly, even though my vision check-up is always fine.

_____ **Total**

ACTIVITY 5: CONTINUED

Kinesthetic Modality

_____ I start a project before reading the directions.
_____ I dislike sitting at a desk for long periods of time.
_____ I use the trial and error approach to problem solving.
_____ I like to read my textbook while riding an exercise bike.
_____ I take frequent study breaks.
_____ I have a difficult time giving step-by-step instructions.
_____ I enjoy sports and do well at several different types of sports.
_____ I prefer first to see something done and then to do it myself.
_____ I use my hands when describing things.
_____ I have to rewrite or type my class notes to reinforce the material.

_____ **Total**

My scoring result

Visual _____

Auditory _____

Kinesthetic _____

What does this mean for you as a…

Learner: _____

_____

Trainer: _____

_____

Instructional Designer: _____

_____

Now update your Learning Journal (page 55)

ACTIVITY 6A: LEARNING STYLE & TASK ASSOCIATION

This chart helps you to further determine your learning style.

1. Read the situation in the left column.
2. Answer the questions in the next three columns as Yes (Y) or No (N).
3. It's acceptable to answer Yes in more than one column.

When you…	Visual		Auditory		Kinesthetic & Tactile	
Spell	Do you try to see the word?		Do you sound out the word or use a phonetic approach?		Do you write the word down to find if it feels right?	
Talk	Do you dislike listening for too long?	Do you use words such as see, picture and imagine?	Do you enjoy listening but are impatient to talk?	Do you use words such as hear, tune and think?	Do you gesture and use expressive movements?	Do you use words such as feel, touch and hold?
Concentrate	Do you become distracted by untidiness or movement?		Do you become distracted by sounds or noises?		Do you become distracted by activity around you?	
Meet Someone Again	Do you forget names but remember faces or remember where you met?		Do you forget faces but remember names or remember what you talked about?		Do you remember best what you did together?	

ACTIVITY 6A: CONTINUED

When you...	Visual	Auditory	Kinesthetic & Tactile
Contact People on Business	Do you prefer direct face-to-face personal meetings?	Do you prefer the telephone?	Do you talk with them while walking or participating in an activity?
Read	Do you like descriptive scenes or pause to imagine the actions?	Do you enjoy dialog and conversation or hear the characters talk?	Do you prefer action stories or are not a keen reader?
Do Something New at Work	Do you like to see demonstrations, diagrams, slides or posters?	Do you prefer verbal instructions or talking about it with someone else?	Do you prefer to jump right in and try it?
Put Something Together	Do you look at the instructions but prefer directions with pictures	Do you ask someone to tell you or talk you through the instructions?	Do you ignore the instructions and figure it out as you go along?
Need Help with a Computer or Device Application	Do you seek out pictures or diagrams?	Do you call the help desk, ask a neighbor, or growl at the computer?	Do you keep trying to do it or try it on another computer or device?

Total Yes Responses: _____

The dominant column indicates your primary learning style.

Adapted from Colin Rose(1987). Accelerated Learning.

Now update your Learning Journal (page 55)

ACTIVITY 6B: LEARNING STYLE IDEAS GENERATION

As a trainer, what can you add to your training to engage each Learning Style? Add two ideas to each Learning Style.

Auditory

Example
- The trainer speaking in front of participants.
- In pairs, ask participants to discuss a section.

Now your turn
-
-

Visual

Example
- In computer training, work slowly through screens, using the projector, or sharing the demo screen.
- Use colorful flipcharts with pictures.
- Use colored handouts with graphics.

Now your turn
-
-

Kinesthetic

Example
- Complete sections of a handout.
- In computer training, have participants use their own computers.
- Physically participate in activities.

Now your turn
-
-

Now update your Learning Journal (page 55)

ADULT LEARNING PRINCIPLE 3
- LEARNING TYPES
- THE 4MAT SYSTEM

PART 4

ADULT LEARNING PRINCIPLES - LEARNING TYPES - THE 4MAT SYSTEM

What is 4Mat?

Developed by Bernice McCarthy in 1979, The 4MAT Method is a natural cycle for delivering instruction of any kind in a way that...

- connects to learners
- provides relevant information
- offers an opportunity for practice
- allows for creative adaptation of material learned.

The 4MAT System provides for understanding the core elements of learning, and provides guidance in how to use theses elements to improve learning effectiveness. 4MAT instruction appeals to ALL learners in turn.

Overview of four Learning Types

The four Learning Types identified by McCarthy are:

Type 1: WHY… Innovative Learners are primarily interested in personal meaning. They need to have reasons for learning – ideally, reasons that connect new information with personal experience and establish the information's usefulness in daily life. Some of the many instructional modes effective with this learner type are cooperative learning, brainstorming, and activities that ask "What's in it for me?"

Type 2: WHAT… Analytic Learners are primarily interested in acquiring facts in order to deepen their understanding of concepts and processes. They are capable of learning effectively from lectures, and enjoy independent research, analysis of data, and hearing what "the experts" have to say.

Type 3: HOW… Common Sense Learners are primarily interested in how things work; they want to "get in and try it." Concrete, experiential learning activities work best for them – using activities, hands-on tasks and Kinesthetic experiences etc.

Type 4: WHAT IF… Dynamic Learners are primarily interested in self-directed discovery. They rely heavily on their own intuition, and seek to teach both themselves and others. Any type of independent study is effective for these learners. They also enjoy simulations, role-play, and learning games.

THE 4MAT MODEL IN MORE DETAIL

People learn in different ways. These differences depend on many things:
- Who we are
- Where we are
- How we see ourselves, and
- What people ask of us.

It simplifies learning behavior and allows you to structure a BALANCED training session, which accommodates all types of learners – regardless of the trainer's own preference for learning.

Bernice McCarthy combined many adult learning theories. These styles are based on the work of Gregorc & Butler (1984) and Kolb (1984). The index of Learning Styles Questionnaire developed by Solomon and Felder (Felder, 1993) provides data relevant to this theory. The Myers-Briggs Type Indicator (MBTI) and the Kiersey Temperament Sorter II define an associated theory for personality style and temperaments.

Why: The Imaginative Learners

Seeks personal meaning. Judges things in relationship to values. Functions through social interaction. Wants to make the world a better place. Is cooperative and sociable. Respects authority, when it is earned.

What: The Analytic Learners

Seeks intellectual competence. Judges things by factual verification. Functions by adapting to experts. Needs to know "the important things," and wants to add to the world's knowledge. Is patient and reflective. Prefers chain-of-command authority.

How: The Common Sense Learners

Seeks solutions to problems. Judges things by their usefulness. Functions through hands-on activities. Wants to make things happen. Is practical and straightforward. Sees authority as necessary, but will work around it if forced.

What if: The Dynamic Learners

Seeks hidden possibilities. Judges things by gut reactions. Functions by synthesizing various parts. Enjoys challenging complacency. Is enthusiastic and adventuresome. Tends to disregard authority.

Complete Activity # 7
Learning Types Ideas Generation

ACTIVITY 7: LEARNING TYPES IDEAS GENERATION

As a trainer, what can you add to your training to engage each Learning Type? Add two ideas to each Learning Type?

Why learners

Example
- At the beginning, tell participants why they need to know the content.
- Ask participants for their own experience with this or similar systems.

Now your turn
- _____
- _____

What learners

Example
- Go through the specific steps, slowly with clarity and precision.
- Give participants handouts with steps, sequence and data presented clearly and with detail.

Now your turn
- _____
- _____

ACTIVITY 7: CONTINUED

How learners

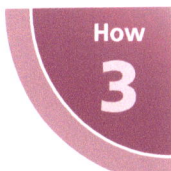

Example
- Practice the steps themselves with only a little guidance from the trainer.
- Fill in the blanks in the participant workbook.
- Show participants how the system works (on the surface and behind the scenes).

Now your turn
-
-

What if learners

Example
- Allow participants to change the rules.
- Create an exercise with missing steps for participants to self-discover the correct procedure.
- Create new ways of doing a task or find the quickest or most efficient way.

Now your turn
-
-

 Download the **Quick Reference Wall Chart** from https://www.catherinematttiske.com/books

HOT TIP: Note this page as a handy reference to help boost your training activity 'Ideas Bank'

Activity 7 - Check your Answers

The following table lists some possibilities for activities for each of the 4Mat quadrants. Compare your answers with each of the lists below. As there are endless possibilities for each 4Mat quadrant ensure that your answers follow each quadrants general theme.

Activating knowledge – To get others interested

- Brainstorming
- WII-FM questions (What's in it for me)
- Demonstrations
- Mind maps
- Make a logo
- Imagery

Gaining knowledge – Teaching factual information

- Lecture
- Charts, graphs etc
- Pictures
- Flowcharts
- Timelines etc
- Examples of the finished product/process
- Step-by-step processes

Using knowledge – Learn by practice

- Hands-on activities
- Worksheets
- Puzzles
- Fact games
- Read given material
- Test theories
- Practice

Applying knowledge – Do something personal with new knowledge

- Write story, poem, journal etc
- Think of how to use in real life
- Likely challenges in real life
- Tips, tricks and traps
- Opportunities to change/modify process

Now update your Learning Journal (page 55)

MAJOR REVIEW

PART 5

SUMMARY OF KEY POINTS

"Get over the idea that only children should spend their time in study. Be a student so long as you still have something to learn, and this will mean all your life."

HENRY L. DOHERTY

As a result of completing this Learning Short-take® you should remember the following key points:

- When training or presenting, you should aim to balance all adult learning styles within your training program or presentation.
- Global learners optimize their learning by knowing the end goal before they begin learning, while specific learners learn best by being confident with each step of learning before they progress.
- When designing training or a presentation consider what participants see, hear and do.
- Engage 'why' learners with the benefit of what you are teaching or presenting. Then, present the content clearly and without variation followed by participants practicing what they have learned. Finally, provide tips, tricks, traps, changes and challenges to the information presented followed by a review to check learning.

 **Complete Activity # 8**
Final Review - True or False

ACTIVITY 8: FINAL REVIEW - TRUE OR FALSE

Answer True (T) or False (F) to the following statements. For false answers correct the statement to make it read as true.

		Answer True (T) or False (F). If the answer is False - correct the statement.
1.	Three Adult Learning Principles are Modalities, Learning Style - Global and Specific, Learning Type - 4Mat.	
2.	During the opening of a course trainers should give the Overview and Goals of the course, particularly for Specific Learners.	
3.	Specific learners may have difficulty in verbalizing process.	
4.	Specific learners are often known as sequential or linear learners.	
5.	The three modalities are Visual, Auditory and Kinesthetic.	
6.	Kinesthetic learners learn best by 'hearing' the material.	
7.	Color coding notes may suit an Auditory learner more than a Visual Learner.	
8.	Using recordings for reading and for lecture notes may suit Auditory learners more than Kinesthetic learners.	
9.	The 4-Mat quadrants, in order, are Why, What, What if and How.	
10.	Handouts with steps, sequences and dates presented clearly and with detail may suit a What learner more than a Why learner.	
11.	Asking WII-FM (what's in it for me) questions may suit a What if learner.	
12.	Writing a journal on how the learning can be put into practice is considered a 'What if' activity.	

Now update your Learning Journal (page 55)

Activity 8 - Answer Key - True or False Review

1.	Three Adult Learning Principles are Modalities, Learning Style – Global and Specific, Learning Type – 4Mat	T
2.	During the opening of a course trainers should give the Overview and Goals of the course, particularly for Specific Learners	F (Global learners)
3.	Specific learners may have difficulty in verbalizing process	F (Global learners)
4.	Specific learners are often known as sequential or linear learners	T
5.	The three modalities are Visual, Auditory and Kinesthetic	T
6.	Kinesthetic learners learn best by 'hearing' the material	F (learn best by doing)
7.	Color coding notes may suit an Auditory learner more than a Visual learner.	F (may suit visual learners)
8.	Using recordings for reading and for lecture notes may suit Auditory learners more than Kinesthetic learners.	T
9.	The 4Mat quadrants, in order, are Why, What, What if and How.	F (Why, What, How, What if)
10.	Handouts with steps, sequences and dates presented clearly and with detail may suit a What learner more than a Why learner.	T
11.	Asking WII-FM (what's in it for me) questions may suit a What if learner.	F (Why learner)
12.	Writing a journal on how the learning can be put into practice is considered a 'What if' activity.	T

Now update your Learning Journal (page 55)

Section 2
LEARNING JOURNAL

The Learning Journal is used throughout the process to record your key learnings, hot tips and things to remember.

Update your Learning Journal at anytime. Ensure you complete your Learning Journal after you finish each activity. Then turn back to the Learning Short-take® to continue your learning.

LEARNING JOURNAL

As you work through this Learning Short-take®, make detailed notes during this program of the lessons you have learned and any useful skill areas. For each lesson or refresher point think about how you could further develop this skill. Your coach will want to discuss these with you in your Skill Development Action Planning meeting.

*"…that is what learning is.
You suddenly understand something you've understood all your life, but in a new way."*

DORIS LESSING

"Act as though it were impossible to fail."

WINSTON CHURCHILL

"The wise do at once what the fool does later."

BALTASAR GRACIAN (1601-58), SPANISH JESUIT PRIEST AND AUTHOR.

Learning or Idea	Action to be taken	Result Expected

Learning Journal - continued

Learning or Idea	Action to be taken	Result Expected

"Anyone who stops learning is old, whether at twenty or eighty."

HENRY FORD

Learning or Idea	Action to be taken	Result Expected

"

Do not be too timid or squeamish about your actions. All life is an experiment. What if you do fail, and get fairly rolled in the dirt once or twice. Up again, you shall never be so afraid of a tumble.

RALPH WALDO EMERSON

Section 3

SKILL DEVELOPMENT ACTION PLAN

Your Skill Development Action Plan is the last Step in the process. After you have completed the Learning Short-take® and all Activities, update your Learning Journal, then complete this section.

SKILL DEVELOPMENT ACTION PLAN

This is the most important part of the program - your individual Skill Development Action Plan.

You need to complete this plan before meeting with your manager or prior to on-going coaching. You will discuss it in detail with your manager or coach as he or she will ensure that you have everything you need to complete the tasks and activities.

Once you have completed your **Skill Development Action Plan** schedule a meeting time with your manager or coach to review your plan. Take your Learning Short-take® and all other documentation received during the training course to this meeting.

Remember - you have committed to your **Skill Development Action Plan**, and need to make time to complete your tasks!

> *"The mind, once stretched by a new idea, never regains its original dimensions."*
>
> OLIVER WENDELL HOLMES

"Imagination is the eye of the soul."

JOSEPH JOUBERT (1754-1824)

Task or activity (Be specific)	Measure (this will help you to know you have achieved it)	Date (Be specific)
Reflect on your Learning Journal. Transfer action items that you can apply to your job. Ensure that you include some 'stretch goals' and also a blend of short, medium and long term goals.	Apart from you, who else is needed to assist you in achieving your goal.	Be specific. A general date such as 'Quarter 1', 'August', or 'by end of year' is vague and more likely to result in not achieving your target. Be specific – e.g. 22nd November.

IDEAS FOR DISCUSSION WITH MY MANAGER

Ideas

CONGRATULATIONS!

You've now completed this Learning Short-take®.

Meet with your Manager/Coach to discuss your
Skill Development Action Plan.

"

*You gain strength, courage, and confidence
by every experience in which you really stop to look fear
in the face...*

*The danger lies in refusing to face the fear,
in not daring to come to grips with it...*

*You must make yourself succeed every time.
You must do the thing you think you cannot do.*

ELEANOR ROOSEVELT

"

QUICK REFERENCE

This Quick Reference provides you with a summary of key concepts, models and reference material from Learning Short-takes®. We have also included some quotations to ponder.

Use this section as a quick reference to keep your learning active.

Quick Reference

It's what you learn after you know it all that counts.

JOHN WOODEN

Three Adult Learning Principles

1. Balance Global and Specific
2. Write for each Learning Type
3. Use Multi-sensory ways of learning for each Learning Style

Quick Reference

> *Success is not for-ever; and failure isn't fatal.*
>
> DON SHULA

Global vs. Specific

Global

- Prefer learning by observing the larger picture
- Learn in chunks
- Are holistic

Specific

- Sequential Learners
- Logical & Stepwise
- Prefer presentation in linear and orderly manner
- Instructions in steps

Quick Reference

> *You learn
> something every day
> if you pay attention.*
>
> RAY LEBLOND

Learning Styles Modalities

Visual
Learn through seeing

Auditory
Learn through listening

Kinesthetic
Learn through moving, doing and touching

Quick Reference

> *Anyone who stops learning is old, whether at twenty or eighty.*
>
> — HENRY FORD

Visual - Learn through seeing

Things to add to training…

- Handouts
- Wallcharts with quotes
- PowerPoint Slideshow
- Color Participant Guides
- Flipcharts with key content
- Draw icon, graphic, symbol activities
- Flipchart activities & present back
- Suitable Pictures & Graphics
- Flowcharts & Diagrams
- Colored Markers
- Video

Quick Reference

Auditory - Learn through listening

Things to add to training...
- Music
- Pair & Share
- Mini-lectures
- Group discussion
- Present Back key learnings
- Guest Speakers
  (Subject Matter Experts)
- Expert Panel
- Interview
- Debate
- Audio

Kinesthetic - Learn through moving, doing and touching

Things to add to training…
- Building Models
- Frequent Breaks
- Whole Group Activities
- Presentation of Key Learnings
- Move participants around room after each break
- Self-discovery (rather than set directions)
- Small Group Activities
- Hands-on activities
- Role Playing

Quick Reference

*Learning is a treasure that will follow
its owner everywhere.*

CHINESE PROVERB

Learning Types 4Mat

Quick Reference

Learning Types

Activating Knowledge
To get others interested

Things to add to training…

- WII-FM questions
- Demonstration
- Mind mapping
- Brainstorming
- Make a logo
- Imagery

Learning Types

Gaining Knowledge
Teaching Factual Information

Things to add to training…

- Lecture
- Timelines
- Charts, graphs
- Example of the finished product
- Step-by-step processes
- Flowcharts
- Pictures

Quick Reference

> *Learning is defined as a change in behavior. You haven't learned a thing until you can take action and use it.*
>
> — DON SHULA AND KEN BLANCHARD

Learning Types

Learn by Practice

Things to add to training…

- Read given material
- Hands-on activities
- Test theories
- Worksheets
- Fact games
- Puzzles
- Practice

Learning Types

Applying Knowledge

Do something personal with new knowledge

Things to add to training…

- Tips, Tricks, Traps
- Personal Action Plan
- Group Action Plan
- Write story or journal
- Brainstorm uses in real life
- Likely challenges in real life
- Opportunities to change/modify process

> *When the student is ready,
> the teacher appears.*
>
> BUDDHIST PROVERB

"

*In real life the greatest heroes are often found among the most ordinary people.
Do not wait for extraordinary circumstances to do good; try to use ordinary situations.*

JEAN PAUL RICHTER

"

NEXT STEPS

Congratulations! You have now completed this Learning Short-take® title. The entire list of Learning Short-takes® can be found on the catherinemattiske.com website.

In this section we have suggested Learning Short-take® titles for you that will build your learning. You may order these Learning Short-takes® online at https://www.catherinemattiske.com/books or from your bookstores.

Adult Learning Principles 2
Blending Interaction with Measurement

Course Content

- Part 1: Fundamentals of Effective Learning
- Part 2: Measurement Myths
- Part 3: Measuring Through Interaction & Review
- Part 4: Learning Activities
- Part 5: Review Activities
- Part 6: Bringing It All Together

Learning Short-take® Outline

Adult Learning Principles 2 combines self-study with realistic workplace activities to develop skills in learning interaction and measurement. Building on Adult Learning Principles 1, this Learning Short-take® examines the importance of demonstrating the impact of learning. It explores common myths of learning measurement and using interaction to support and measure learning. For learning designers, trainers, educators, facilitators, and managers the library of training activities provided allow you to develop new and innovative strategies to assess learning during workshops, courses, sessions, and eLearning modules.

In the corporate world, measuring and demonstrating the value of learning is discussed frequently. Organizations are searching for the perfect way to link human resource capability and learning outcomes with business strategy. To achieve this result, it is important to know how to effectively deploy and measure learning. During the learning itself we have the greatest opportunity to observe learning transfer taking place.

Adult Learning Principles 2 provides practical know-how and a library of activities that can be used to measure learning during any learning experience. It features **Mattiske's Training Focus Model** and includes the **Training Review Analysis Tool** as a free download.

Learning Objectives

- Know the underlying drivers of successful learning outcomes
- Identify common myths about measuring learning
- Recognize the value of Interaction and Review for better learning measurement
- Define the levels of participant interaction and adopt a mindset for interaction in learning
- List the different types of learning activities
- Identify and explain the different types of Review
- Collect a bank of practical learning and review activities
- Create a Skill Development Action Plan

Adult Learning Principles 3
Advanced Adult Learning Principles

Course Content

- Part 1: Whole Brain Learning
  - Brain Dominance
  - Assessing Hemispheric Dominance

- Part 2: Multiple Intelligences
  - Logical-Mathematical Intelligence
  - Musical Intelligence
  - Bodily-Kinesthetic Intelligence
  - Visual/Spatial Intelligence
  - Interpersonal Intelligence
  - Intrapersonal Intelligence
  - Naturalist Intelligence
  - Existential Intelligence

- Part 3: The Metacognitive Process
  - Strategies for Developing Metacognitive Behaviors
  - Journal Writing

Learning Short-take® Outline

Adult Learning Principles 3 combines self-study with realistic workplace activities to build advanced knowledge of adult learning principles. Building on Adult Learning Principles 1 and 2, it explores three sophisticated principles of adult learning: Multiple Intelligences, Whole Brain Learning and Metacognitive Reflection. **Adult Learning Principles 3** is designed for educators, trainers and facilitators who work in instructor-led training, e-Learning, distance learning, self-study and other types of learning interventions.

The reliance on just a few training approaches may be a combination of trainer "comfort" and organizational expectations. Often, corporate training represents a school-like environment: lectures followed with an activity. With increasing pressure on training departments to reduce training session duration and convert instructor led training to e-learning, trainers must adopt new ways of delivering learning. This Learning Short-take® will provide a plethora of new ideas and refuel the way you design learning.

Learning Objectives

- Explain the value of using a balanced adult learning approach.
- List the characteristics of left brain dominance vs. right brain dominance.
- Use the Brain Dominance theory to analyze and make improvements to an existing training program.
- List the Multiple Intelligences.
- Analyze an existing training program and suggest improvements to maximize the Multiple Intelligence Balance.
- Define metacognitive reflection and be able to implement learning and review activities using this training method.
- Create a Skill Development Action Plan.

Creative Business Thinking
Developing the Skills for Thinking Outside the Box

Learning Short-take® Outline

Creative Business Thinking includes a library of brilliant creativity tools, fun activities, and challenging business scenarios. These will help to stretch your thinking by deliberately challenging existing perspectives and considering alternative ways of working.

Creative Business Thinking is packed with techniques for creative thinking and fun 'mind quiz' activities. **Creative Business Thinking** constructively challenges the status quo to enable new ideas to surface and solve problems in ways that may not initially come to mind.

Within each of us there exists an infinite capacity for creating ideas and nurturing them through to innovation. **Creative Business Thinking** emphasizes pragmatic tools and techniques to successfully unlock creative potential.

Creative Business Thinking includes the job aid **15 Creativity Techniques for Problem Solving**, and the **Creative Business Thinking Techniques Wall Chart**, provided to you as free downloadable tools.

Learning Objectives

- Undertake a self assessment in creativity.
- List personal and organizational creative contributions.
- Choose personal creative techniques to be used in the workplace.
- Match group creativity techniques with case study applications.
- Use six thinking hats to solve a business challenge.
- Create a plan for an upcoming team meeting employing creative thinking techniques.

Course Content

- Part 1: Creativity and lateral thinking
- Part 2: Unleash those creative forces
- Part 3: Personal creative thinking techniques
- Part 4: Tools for Creative Business Thinking
  - 6 thinking hats
  - Brainstorming
  - Metaphors
  - Cause & effect (Fishbone Diagram)
  - Work breakdown structure
  - 5-Why's
  - Different point of view
  - Concept mapping / Mind mapping
- Part 5: Answers

www.ingramcontent.com/pod-product-compliance
Lightning Source LLC
Chambersburg PA
CBHW040002110526
44587CB00001BA/22